Walk Cornwall
Lizard Point
Coverack, Cadgwith & Kynance

GW00890278

The old serpentine factory at Poltesco.

Lizard Point & the far south
Coverack, Cadgwith, Lizard Point & Kynance

THIS IS THE LIZARD at its most undiluted and unrestrained – a very impressive landscape quite unlike anything else in Cornwall. It gets its distinctive character from the unusual serpentine bedrock which alternates with pink Kennack Gneiss and the handsome crags and cliffs of the schists around **Landewednack**. The coast is a parade of beautiful coves and beaches – **Downas**, **Carleon**, **Housel**, **Pentreath** and **Kynance** – as well as a roll call of fearsome cliffs. The first real taste of serpentine scenery comes south of Coverack on the cliffs at **Black Head**. Between **Kennack Sands** and **Landewednack** the cliffs are interspersed with small coves and shallow wooded valleys like **Gwendreath** and **Poltesco** that stretch up onto **Goonhilly Downs**. It's a coastline of tiny isolated beaches once popular with smugglers.

Lizard Point takes the full brunt of gales that spin and spiral north from the Equator. Floundering sailing ships were once driven onto the reefs and into the high cliffs. Hundreds of wrecks and thousands of bodies have been washed ashore on this coast. Any cliff that has soil deep enough to hold a shallow grave has been pressed into service. At **Pystyll Ogo** the little beach is full of beautiful pebbles – sparkling black basalt, grey and blue varieties of schist and the salt and pepper colouring of Man O'War Gneiss.

On the west coast from **Pentreath** to **Kynance Cove**, heathland reaches down to cloak the cliff slopes. In the summer the grassy cliffs are full of the colours of nodding *Harebells*, varieties of clover on the schist soils and a seaside riot of daisies and *Bird's-foot Trefoil*. It's a multicoloured rebuke to the sombre and brooding serpentine cliffs.

GETTING AROUND
BUS
This section is served by two bus routes from Helston. The Helston - Lizard Town bus (**37**) via Mullion & the main beaches. The Helston - St Keverne & Coverack bus (**36**) also goes past Goonhilly Earth Station & Traboe Cross.

Serpentine workshop at Lizard Point

HIGHLIGHTS...
- Heath in bloom in July & August on Lizard & Predannack Downs
- Boat trips from Mullion Cove, Coverack & Cadgwith

PLACES TO VISIT
- Lizard Lighthouse Heritage Centre
- Lizard Wireless Station

PLACES TO EAT
- Coverack has a pub, cafes & restaurants
- Cadgwith has a cafe & food at the pub with singing on Fridays & beach barbecues in the summer
- Cafe at Kynance Cove

Walks 1 & 2

Coverack, Lowland Point, Roskilly's & The Manacles

Ice creams, prehistoric pots & sacred crags

Helston

St Keverne

Coverack

Lizard Point

BUS

Helston - Coverack - St Keverne bus. Coverack bus shelter. or St Keverne stops.

CAR PARKING

Car park (& loos) at North Corner & small car park at Dolor Point (both Coverack). There's also parking for visitors to Roskilly's & some roadside parking at Treglohan plus a few spaces at Giant's Quoit & near Dean Quarry.

FOOD & DRINK

Roskilly's for ice creams, teas & meals. Coverack has the Bay Hotel & Paris Hotel (seaside beer garden) & cafes. Food shop at the General Stores in Coverack & in St Keverne.

LOOK OUT FOR...

- Watch milking & ice cream making at Roskilly's plus Long Meadow Nature Trail
- Picnic & wild flowers at Lowland Point
- Pebbles in Coverack Cove
- Coverack Windsurf Centre

Coverack is a place of many pleasures. It's a mecca for geologists who come to study the rocks on **Mill Beach** – pebble heaven – and for botanists who come to study the plants on the way to **Lowland Point** – a flower heaven. You might enjoy a windsurf in the bay, a stroll around the harbour with an ice cream, to browse the craft shops or sit with a drink in the seaside beer garden of the Paris Hotel.

Coverack

This is the last naturally sheltered harbour until St Michael's Mount. The pier has a charming enclosing arm very much like the Old Pier at Newlyn. In the C19th this was a big pilchard fishery as the handsome pilchard cellars behind the Paris Hotel show. The pilchard shoals have long since left but a fleet of small boats work from here sharing the harbour with windsurfers, canoeists and dinghy sailors. A lifeboat was stationed in Coverack until 1963 because of the danger of the **Manacles**. At high water the reef is all but invisible but as the tide drops you can almost hear a snarl as the rocks emerge like bared teeth.

Roskilly's

Tregellast Barton, just south of St Keverne village,

is the home of wonderful Roskilly's Ice Cream. There are craft shops, a restaurant and you can watch the ice cream being made. A trail follows the stream down the valley past wildlife pools to Godrevy Cove.

Lowland Point & Carrick Crane Crags

The walk from North Corner to Lowland Point in the late spring and summer is a Lizard highlight. It's famous for the range and number of flowers. The crags above Lowland Point seem to have had a significance for the Stone Age inhabitants of this area. Neolithic pottery from about 4,000 years ago was discovered in a cave below Carrick Crane Rock in 1918. This type of pottery, called *Grooved Ware*, is associated with monuments like henges and with burial sites in southern England and therefore seems to have had some ritual importance. We know from other sites that caves were important places for ritual in the Stone Age and similar fragments of Grooved Ware have been found in the crevices at Logan Rock on the Land's End peninsula. The opening at Carrick Crane rock is visible (but a scramble) and it's worth a detour from the coast path. The sherds are in the Royal Cornwall Museum.

Below & left
The *SS Ocklinge* hard & fast on Lowland Point in March 1932. The Captain dumped part of the cargo of iron ore overboard in an attempt to float her off the reef. It's still there scattered between the boulders slowly rusting away (*photo left*). It didn't work & she became a total loss.

Giant's
Quoits

Trevallack Laddenvean Well Lane

Parc-an-grouse

Rosenithon
(No parking)

St Keverne School Hill Little Orchard
Treginges

Porthoustock
Stream

Coast path
heads inland at
Godrevy Cove

Long Meadow
Nature Trail

Trelyn Tregellast
Barton

Trethance

Godr
Cov

Treskewe Roskilly's

Treglohan

Walk 1
Roskilly's Stroll
• 3.1km (2 miles)
• 1–2 hours

Dean
Quarry
(gabbro,
disused)

De
Po

SS Fo
1919

Chywoone

B3293

Trevean

Short cut
to Roskilly's

Polcries
Beach

SS Gap
1928

Trebarveth

Dispatch
1809

Main Dale

Trevalsoe

Boscarnon

The
Grove

Carrick
Crane
Rock

Lowlan

Glenbe
Great W
Ockling e

Gilly Tregod
(abandoned farm)

Carrick Crane Crags

Mina Cantaquin
1955

The Oar

B3294

Kilter

Davas

Pedn-myin
Affleck 1838

North
Corner

Gabbro
(Oceanic crust)

Trebarveth Romano-British
salt works. Easy to miss on
the cliff edge the remains
of ovens to evaporate salt
water. The Cornish Sea Salt
Company do a similar
thing today at Porthkerris.

Coverack
bus shelter

The Bay

Coverack Cove

Transition Zone
Mohorovičić discontinuity

Mill
Beach

Dolor Point

Serpentine
(Upper Mantle)

Paris Hotel

erack

Archangelos 1929

nmarth YHA
Farm Sch

Perprean Cove

The Oxen
Rose 1866

Chynhalls
Farm

Omer Denise 1932

Polgravel
Pindos 1912

Walk 2
Lowland Point
• 8.2km (5 miles)
• 3–4 hours

Headlands

Guthens

Walk
3

Mears
Beach

Chynhalls
(Mear) Point

Porthbeer
Cove

Serpentine
(Upper Mantle)

0	0.25km	0.5km	0.75km	1km
0	¼ mile		½ mile	

Lûz
Manacle Pt
Mildran's
Rock
Dulgevean
Rocks

Gabbro

Maen Garrick
Sarah Jane 1823

Gwinges
Princess Charlotte 1802

Gabbro fractured
by numerous
black dykes

Manacles

Vase Rock
Rose 1838

Penwin Reef

Manacles
bell buoy

MS Primrose 1809 with
e loss of 120 only one
rvivor - a drummer
by. Lost on the same
ght as the Dispatch
Lowland Point

Minstrel
Rock

Spyridion Vagliano 1890

Mohegan wrecked 1898
with the loss of 106

Cabinet 1872

Maen Varses or The Voices
Carn-du Rocks

SS Juno 1915

Mormon Maid 1851

en
nd

hn wrecked 1855 with the
s of 120 lives (buried in
Keverne Churchyard)

John & Rebecca 1867

e transport ship Dispatch, with a detachment
the 7th Hussars, returning home from the
ninsular War wrecked on Lowland Point with
e loss of 104, only 7 survived.

Wra

The Paris is grounded

The *City of Paris* was one of the swiftest steam ships
ever built – a three times winner of the Blue Riband
for the fastest Atlantic crossing. In May 1899 she ran
aground on Lowland Point having lost her way in fog.
Miraculously, she must have steamed straight through
the Manacles past the *Mohegan* – wrecked only a few
months before with the loss of 106. Many victims were
still entombed inside the ship with only the tolling
of the Manacles bell buoy for company (it still tolls
today). Thankfully for the *Paris* there was only a slight
sea running and all her passengers and crew were
saved, in dreadful contrast to the heavy loss of life on
the *Mohegan*. The *Paris* was pulled free and towed to
Belfast for repair, resuming service as the
SS Philadelphia.

The Paris grounded on Lowland Point,
in the foreground the masts of the Mohegan.

Walks 3 & 4

Coverack, Black Head & Downas Cove

Black cliffs of the east coast

BUS

Helston - Coverack - St Keverne bus. Coverack bus shelter stop at North Corner. Instead of returning to Coverack on a circular walk you can pick up the bus again at Kuggar above Kennack Sands on the Helston - Lizard Town service. That would make an 8.5km one way walk from Coverack bus shelter at North Corner.

CAR PARKS

Large car park at North Corner, small car park at Dolor Point (both Coverack). Small National Trust parking area at Treleaver (4 or 5 cars only).

FOOD & DRINKS

Paris Hotel (seaside beer garden) & cafes in Coverack. Food shop at the General Stores in Coverack.

LOOK OUT FOR...

- Shoot the breeze at Downas Cove
- Swim at Mears Beach
- Picnic on Chynhalls Point or Downas Cove
- Boat trip from the harbour at Coverack

As you walk south from Coverack towards **Chynhalls** you can be in no doubt you have left the Meneage. Gone are the intimate wooded creeks and rich farmland. For the first time you encounter the scenery of serpentine. Crags glower down at you as you walk past **Perprean** and **Polgravel**. This is an altogether less soft and contented landscape. The cliffs build towards **Black Head** and **Pedn Boar** then ease down towards the beach at **Downas Cove**. It's a taste of what's in store on the more exposed serpentine cliffs of the west coast – the magnificent black cliffs of Vellan Head and The Rill.

Chynhalls Point & cliff castle

This is one of two cliff castles on this stretch of coast, the other is at nearby Lankidden. The earth ramparts are clearly visible. We know from excavations at other sites that the ramparts often had timber palisades on top of the bank. They date from the later part of the Iron Age, which seems to have been a time of increased piracy and raiding. They may have been pressed back into use when the Saxons and Vikings invaded eastern and northern England pushing many Britons before them – a cause of the great Celtic migrations to Brittany in the C5th and C6th.

Downas Cove

The valley behind is beautiful on a summer day and it's a good place to stop and do a bit of prospecting on the strand line. Sand is exposed for an hour or two each side of low water when there's a chance to paddle in the sandy pools and examine the serpentine where the sand and sea have polished the rock. The south-facing cliffs teem with butterflies.

0	0.25km	0.5km	0.75km	1km
0		¼ mile	½ mile	

Downas Cove

Map Labels

Penhallick Farm

Coverack

Dolor Point

Paris Hotel

Archangelos 1929

Trevothen

Penmarth Farm Sch

YHA

Perprean Cove

Little Trevothen

The Oxen

Rose 1866

Cold War nuclear bunker

Chynhalls Farm

Omer Denise 1932

Polgravel

Pindos 1912

Pendnavounder

Headlands

Guthens

Trewillis

Mears Beach

Chynhalls (Mear) Point

Porthbeer Cove

Walk 4
Black Head
• 6.3km (4 miles)
• 3–4 hours

Treleaver Cottage

Chynhalls Cliff

Walk 3
Chynhalls Stroll
• 2.6km (1½ miles)
• 1–2 hours

Treleaver

Tremorna

Old copper mine workings in cliff

Goldolphin 1888

Downas Cove

Wreathe

Eagles Point

Meludjack

Eagles Cove

Ebber Rocks

Plantagenet 1897

Briel 1792

Beagles Hole

Treleaver Cliff

Old lookout

The Bees

Dinas Cove

Gunvor 1912

Hyrlas Rock

Black Head

Dispatch 1809

Clan Alpine 1873

Pedn Boar

9

Walk 5

Kennack Sands & Lankidden Cove

Childhood memories & cliff castles

Helston

Coverack

Lankidden
Kennack Sands

Lizard Point

BUS
Helston - Lizard Town bus. Kuggar stop is about 15mins walk from Kennack Sands. You can also pick up the Helston - St Keverne bus at Coverack (8.5km) or by walking north over Goonhilly Downs to pick it up at Traboe Cross or the Earth Station stop (about a 6km walk).

CAR PARKS
There's a large car park at Kennack Sands – always busy on sunny days in the school holidays.

FOOD & DRINKS
Kennack Sands has a couple of beach shops.

LOOK OUT FOR...
- Poldowrian Garden & museum (open on occasional days in spring & summer)
- Pond dipping behind Kennack Sands
- Shingle plants at the top of the beach
- Picnic at Lankidden Cliff Castle & a swim at Lankidden Cove
- Inland walks onto Goonhilly Downs

As well as the beach, which is the most popular on this side of the Lizard, there's plenty to explore at Kennack Sands with cliff walks in either direction and the chance to walk inland onto **Goonhilly Downs**. We've highlighted a short walk to **Lankidden Cove** where you can picnic inside the cliff castle or, if the tide is out, at the cove below.

Kennack Sands
This is a great beach for families and a good place for inexperienced body boarders and surfers because it's less exposed to big Atlantic swells than the west coast beaches like Poldhu. For beachcombers, there are plenty of interesting pebbles – serpentine and pink Kennack Gneiss are the most colourful. The reedy pool at the back of the beach has boardwalks so the children can go pond dipping in the summer and it's often buzzing with dragonflies. Basking sharks frequently swim in close to the cliffs here.

Lankidden Cove
This is one of those lovely little sandy coves that you occasionally chance upon when you're walking the cliffs. If you're lucky, the tide will be out as the beach is only uncovered for a few hours each side of low water. It's a bit of a scramble down.

Lankidden Cliff Castle
An obvious defensive site protected on the landward side by some impressive earth ramparts. It seems unlikely that it was a permanent settlement because it has no water supply and it's so exposed (just like Chynhalls). Some cliff castles are known to have been used as trading places but most are thought to have functioned as temporary refuges from Irish and Viking raiders. They usually date to around the last part of the Iron Age (2,700 years ago).

Kennack Sands with the Caerverracks reef in the middle distance.
Eastern Cliffs, Lankidden & Pedn Boar in the background.

arrow
Croft

Serpentine

Ponsongath

Genter
Farm

Access
point

Gwenter

Ponsongath
Farm

Trelea
Comm

The Barrow

Carnpessack

Arrowan
Vean

Goonvean
Farm

Arrowan
Common

Arrowan

Gwendreath
Quarry
(serpentine,
disused)

Trevenwith
Farm

Poldowrian
Garden & Museum
(occasional open days)

Poldowrian

Wild
Acres

Carn
Spernic

Lankidden
Cove

ack
ds

Eastern Cliffs

Spernic
Cove

The Parlour

Serpentine

Kennack
Towans
Caerverracks
Reef

Eastern
Beach

Green
Saddle
Rock

Compass
Cove

Ship's boiler
visible at
low tide

SS Normand 1914

The Jay

Kennack
Sands

Serpentine

Gabbro

Carrick Lûz

Crig-a-tanna Rocks

Serpentine

Walk 5
Lankidden Stroll
• 4.7km (3 miles)
• 1–2 hours

Lankidden
Iron Age Cliff Castle

| 0 | 0.25km | 0.5km | 0.75km | 1km |

| 0 | ¼ mile | ½ mile |

Walks 6 & 7

Goonhilly Downs
Stargazing & solitude

BUS
Helston - Mawgan - Coverack - St Keverne service. Goonhilly stop. Helston - Lizard Town service. Mullion Holiday Village stop on the west side of the downs, 3.9km (2½ miles) from Goonhilly.

CAR PARKING
National Nature Reserve car park at Goonhilly plus small lay-bys at Croft Pascoe & Bray's Cot for those who want to wander the Downs.

FOOD & DRINKS
Nothing in this immediate area but pub & food shops in St Keverne & Mullion plus the Wheel Inn at Cury Cross Lanes.

LOOK OUT FOR...
- Best in the late summer when the downs are dry & the heather & gorse are in flower
- Follow the stream from Goonhilly to Erisey & then down to Poltesco Cove
- Pools full of tadpoles in January at Croft Pascoe Forest

I suspect opinion has always been sharply divided over Goonhilly – you either like it or you don't. For some, it's a bleak and dreary waste fit only for witches, ghosts and highway robbers. For others, it's an exhilarating, strange and absorbing place. Whatever your view, it is without doubt the spiritual heart of the Lizard and one of the few places in Cornwall where you can taste silence and solitude.

Its strangeness comes partly from the contrast between the satellite dishes of the Earth Station and the heathland. But stranger still is the realisation that the Earth Station sits on the focal point of a huge prehistoric ritual landscape that extends in all directions and whose boundaries reach as far as Predannack Downs, Kynance Heights and Barrow Croft – all of which are great walks from here. An array of invisible threads tie groups of barrows back to **Dry Tree** menhir and **Cruc Drænoc** (Cornish: *cruc* is *barrow* and *dreynek* is *thorny*). Barrows (man-made earth mounds) are usually, but not always, associated with the burial of an individual.

The Lizard is, at one and the same time, remarkable for its prehistoric monuments and

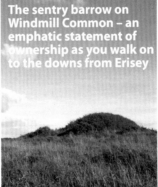

The sentry barrow on Windmill Common – an emphatic statement of ownership as you walk on to the downs from Erisey

oddly missing types found elsewhere in Cornwall. Where are the early prehistoric monuments, the circles, entrance graves and quoits that populate the neighbouring Land's End Peninsula? Perhaps the Lizard

Goonhilly Earth Station

was too thinly populated then or the hunter gatherer lifestyle continued here while pioneer farmers (and their monuments) got going on the moors of Penwith. Whatever the reason, by the time of the later Bronze Age, about 4,000 years ago, the downs were heavily populated with barrows. These people had a fascination with the stars and the seasons possibly because they were skilled mariners. I think the Bronze Age kings would have approved of the huge satellite dishes sending messages to deep space missions while they lay in their barrows staring up at the stars attempting to do the same.

The best way to arrive on the downs is on foot from the coast either by **Erisey** or from **Kennack Sands**. It's often difficult walking, invariably boggy even in summer. As you leave the last trees and stream behind you're presented with a tall 'sentry' barrow on Windmill Common, one of the tallest but least visited.

Flora

Most of the Downs are National Nature Reserves. Goonhilly is a classic for the Lizard flora. Around the area of the National Nature Reserve car park you'll find information boards & all the plants of the serpentine heaths – *Saw-wort, Great Burnet (below), Cornish Heath.*

Above
Dry Tree Menhir. A Bronze Age standing stone at the geographical & spiritual heart of the Lizard. It's a gabbro rock presumably chosen & hauled here from the boulders on Crousa Downs – about 3 miles away. Excavations elsewhere in Britain have uncovered Bronze Age ropes made from Honeysuckle stems.

Below
World War 2 anti-glider defences on Goonhilly Downs. The bases once held upright poles.

Cruc Drænoc & the Dry Tree menhir

Dry Tree is the highest point on the Downs and the central point not only in the prehistoric landscape – burial mounds surround and radiate from here – but the meeting point of five parishes and the site of public hangings, particularly of highwaymen. It is said, mostly in pubs late at night, that the ghosts of highwaymen hanged at Dry Tree still haunt the downs preying on any person foolish enough to venture across the downs at night. At night a ghostly white ship with billowing sails may be seen floating on Croft Pascoe Pool.

RAF Dry Tree

This was an early warning station for RAF Predannack during World War 2 and part of a long chain of radar installations along the south coast of Britain including a similar one at nearby Trelanvean. The brick buildings around the National Nature Reserve car park are associated with it and you can walk onto the roof of the receiver block where there are information boards and you can get wide views across the downs.

Goonhilly Earth Station

The Earth Satellite Station continues the long tradition of communications installations on the Lizard, pioneered by the maritime telegraph station at Bass Point and the transatlantic radio station at Poldhu. Built in the early 1960s, it was for many years the busiest and largest satellite station on Earth, relaying millions of telephone calls, television links and internet services every day. That role has ended and the site is now likely to be used for deep space communication with spacecraft and as a space research centre.

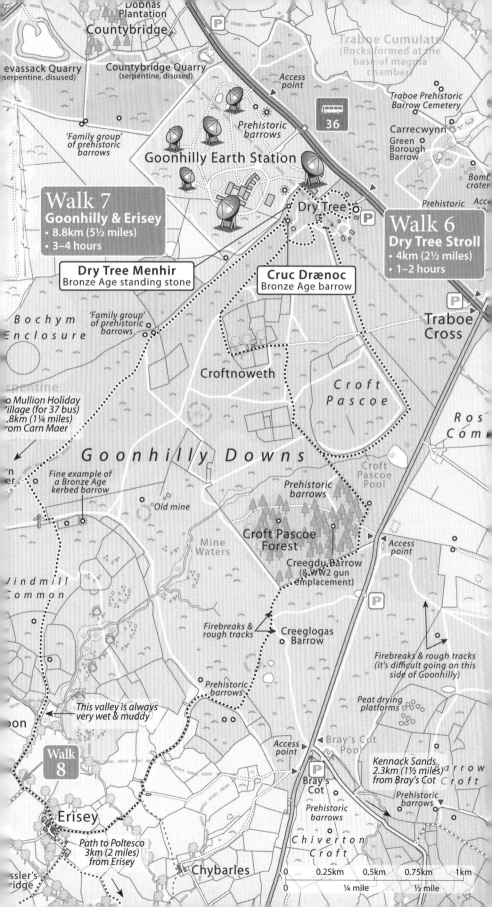

Dobnas
Plantation
Countybridge

Traboe Cumulate
(Rocks formed at the
base of magma
chamber)

evassack Quarry
(serpentine, disused)

Countybridge Quarry
(serpentine, disused)

Access
point

Traboe Prehistoric
Barrow Cemetery

Prehistoric
barrows

Carrecwynn

'Family group'
of prehistoric
barrows

36

Green
Borough
Barrow

Goonhilly Earth Station

Bomb
crater

Prehistoric

Acc

Dry Tree

Walk 7
Goonhilly & Erisey
- 8.8km (5½ miles)
- 3–4 hours

Walk 6
Dry Tree Stroll
- 4km (2½ miles)
- 1–2 hours

Dry Tree Menhir
Bronze Age standing stone

Cruc Drænoc
Bronze Age barrow

Traboe
Cross

B o c h y m
E n c l o s u r e

'Family group'
of prehistoric
barrows

Croftnoweth

C r o f t
P a s c o e

Ros
Com

entine

o Mullion Holiday
illage (for 37 bus)
.8km (1¼ miles)
om Carn Maer

G o o n h i l l y   D o w n s

Croft
Pascoe
Pool

Prehistoric
barrows

Fine example of
a Bronze Age
kerbed barrow

Old mine

Croft Pascoe
Forest

Access
point

Mine
Waters

Windmill
Common

Creegdu Barrow
(& WW2 gun
emplacement)

Firebreaks &
rough tracks

Creeglogas
Barrow

Firebreaks & rough tracks
(it's difficult going on this
side of Goonhilly)

Peat drying
platforms

Prehistoric
barrows

This valley is always
very wet & muddy

Prehistoric
barrows

Access
point

Bray's Cot
Pool

arrow
Croft

Walk 8

Access
point

Bray's
Cot

Kennack Sands
2.3km (1½ miles)
from Bray's Cot

Prehistoric
barrows

Erisey

Prehistoric
barrows

Path to Poltesco
3km (2 miles)
from Erisey

C h i v e r t o n
C r o f t

ssler's
ridge

Chybarles

| 0 | 0.25km | 0.5km | 0.75km | 1km |
| 0 | | ¼ mile | ½ mile | |

Coverack Harbour with Lowland Point in the background.

Walks
8 & 9

Lizard Point & the far south

Poltesco, Carleon Cove, Cadgwith & Erisey

Fish & saints

BUS

Helston - Lizard Town bus. At the top of the walk, get off at Mullion Holiday Village & walk 1.8km (1¼ miles) down the country road to Erisey. At the bottom of the walk, get off at Ruan Minor or Kuggar stops. If you keep going on to the downs from Erisey you can pick up the Helston - St Keverne bus at Goonhilly or Traboe Cross.

CAR PARKS

National Trust car park at Poltesco, small lay-by at Polstangey Bridge. Large public car park above Cadgwith. Avoid driving down the hill from Ruan Minor through Cadgwith village - it's very narrow & steep with lots of bottlenecks.

FOOD & DRINKS

Cadgwith Cove Hotel (pub) & cafe in Cadgwith Beach barbecues in the summer.

LOOK OUT FOR...

- Pebbles at Poltesco
- Singing at the Cadgwith Cove Hotel
- Beach barbecues at Cadgwith

Like all the valleys on the east side of the Lizard, **Ruan Valley**, in which **Cadgwith** sits, and **Poltesco Valley** are hollowed out of the Kennack Gneiss. The soil is noticeably more fertile here than on the surrounding sea of serpentine. We've picked out a very enjoyable walk from **Carleon Cove** to **Erisey** where you are within touching distance of Goonhilly Downs. As you progress up the valley from Poltesco, the vegetation is slowly stripped away until you're standing on the magnificently bleak downs – totally exhilarating.

Poltesco & Carleon Cove

Poltesco Stream has its source all the way up on Goonhilly at Croft Pascoe Pool. It's cut a path down to the sea at Carleon Cove where the pebbly beach creates a natural dam and freshwater pool. The beach has great pebbles – fresh dark green serpentine and a weathered, dark red variety, mottled gabbro and pink Kennack Gneiss, all conveniently polished by the sea. Look out for the *Purple Loosestrife* that grows on the banks of the pool. The Lizard Serpentine Company set up a factory here in 1853, reusing some old fish cellars and the capstan house. A water-powered saw was used to cut and polish serpentine stone, a

fashionable facing for ornate shop fronts, banking halls and wealthy drawing rooms in the City of London. It was a relatively short lived fashion and within 45 years demand had faded away and the factory closed.

Poltesco

18

Cadgwith Cove

Cadgwith Village

This is a favourite of many visitors. Everything is centred around the small cove. Within 20 metres there's a pub, tea house, gallery, fish shop and a shop with ice creams and gifts. You can buy a necklace or a lobster; a painting or a pint. It's better shopping than Harvey Nichols and after you've shopped yourself to exhaustion you can sit and watch the boats unload their catches on the beach or, sit on the grassy Todden and watch gig boat practice in the bay. The local pub is known throughout West Cornwall for the singing of Cornish songs on a Friday night and there are barbecues on the beach in the summer.

Trenoon

Paths onto Goonhilly Downs

Bray's Cot Pool

Access point

Walk 7

Prehistoric barrows

Bray's Cot

Prehistoric barrows

Bar Cro

Erisey

Kennack Gneiss

Chiverton Croft

Chybarles

Tussler's Bridge

Gweal Goose

Chiverton

Chapel Stile

Cargey Gate

Trerise

Crouder's Bridge

Gwendreath

Parc-an-crouse

Silver Sands Holiday Park

Gwendreath Holiday Park

Path to Eglos Farm café & Ruan Major Church (ruin)

Kingey

Friar's Lane

KG

Kennac Sands

Tresaddern

Namparra

Pons Medda

Crowgey Farm

Kuggar

Chy Carne

Sea Acres Park

Corgerrick

Kennack Sands Park

Cavouga

Polbream

Serpentine

Walk 8
Erisey
5.8km (3½ miles)
2–3 hours

Treal

KG

Treveddon Farm

Polstangey Farm

Poltesco Farm

Little Cove

Todden

Poltesco Ro

Carleon (Poltesco) Cove

Black Rock

Serpentine

37

Treleague

Mill

Poltesco

orner

Treleague Crossroads

Poltesco Lane

Friar's Lane

Carleon

SS Highland Flin 1907

Ruan Valley

Walk 9
Poltesco Stroll
• 1.6km (1 mile)
• 1 hour

St Ruan

Sch

Ruan Minor

Ledgeventon

Enys Head

Brandise

Kildown Cove

Signal Staff Quar (serpentine, disused)

Bruggan

Steep, narrow road (avoid in summer)

New Road

Kildown Point

GOONHILLY SH

St Ruan's Well
Medieval Holy Well

Terrick
The Colt

Huers Hut

MAN O' WAR SHE 500 million year rocks that predate creation of the R Ocean

Chyheira Farm

Cadgwith

Fishing Cove

The Todden

Little Cove (Swimming Cove)

St Grada's Church

Prazegooth Lane

Devil's Frying Pan (Collapsed cave)

Anvoaze

Gwavas Vean

Prazegooth

Ynyswidden

Serpentine

Gwavas Farm

Dollar Ogo

Chough's Ogo

Carn Barrow

Schist crags & cliffs

Socoa stranded 1906

Trethvas Farm

Polgwidden

Polbarrow Arch

Craggan Rocks

The Devil's Frying Pan

The Cornish is Hugga Dridgee (Cornish, *ogo* is *cave* and *trig* is *ebb* or *low tide*). It's a cave that has had its roof collapse. This one has been here for at least 400 years. The Lion's Den is a more recent example. Water swirls around the entrance on a high tide.

Erisey Barton

Old farmers will tell you that you can tell the fertility of the land by the quality of the farm buildings. Nowhere is this more true than at Erisey, which is a superb old manor house set in the fertile Poltesco Valley.

St Ruan

The withdrawal of Rome from Britain in AD410 precipitated a period of great population movement in the early Dark Ages. As part of that movement in the C5th and C6th, Christian saints arrived in Cornwall from Ireland and Wales. As they travelled across Cornwall they founded sacred sites, often taking over Iron Age rounds as at Merther Uny, sometimes making an oval *lann* enclosure as at Manaccan and St Anthony. Many Cornish churches now appear to be in odd, isolated places – but it's simply that they were established before towns even existed. St Ruan is a particular favourite on the Lizard. He's said to have lived in a small cell on Goonhilly Downs and to have been magically invulnerable to the wolves who roamed there. In fact, tradition sometimes has him as a werewolf – although this might be a mistranslation, he might simply have been a hairy individual. He was responsible for finally driving the wolves out altogether. Two churches are dedicated to him, Ruan Major, which is now abandoned but within walking distance of Erisey, and the church at Ruan Minor near Cadgwith. His relics were venerated at Ruan Lanihorne.

Above
This barn at Erisey has been faced with blocks of serpentine ashlar in a restrained Georgian classical style. It's actually one of few buildings on the Lizard that uses serpentine as a decorative stone. Undoubtedly the finest building on the Lizard peninsula.
Below
St Ruan's Holy Well near Cadgwith. The structure is probably from the C18th but the site may well date to when St Ruan roamed here, 1,500 years ago.

Walk 10

Lizard Point & the far south

Landewednack, Bass Point, Housel Bay & Lizard Point
A beautiful bay

Helston

Poltesco
Landewednack
Lizard Point

BUS
Helston - Lizard Town bus, Lizard Town or Cross Common stops plus Ruan Minor above Cadgwith.

CAR PARKS
National Trust car park at Lizard Point. There's a limited amount of free parking on Lizard Green & about 10 spaces by Landewednack Church.

FOOD & DRINKS
Lizard Town has cafes, a food shop & pub. Housel Bay Hotel does teas & meals.

LOOK OUT FOR...
- Choughs on the cliffs
- *Fringed Rupture-wort* on the coast path by the lighthouse
- Swim at Housel Bay
- Lizard Wireless Station – run by the National Trust & open at peak summer times
- The Lighthouse Centre

We turn the corner from the sheltered east coast cliffs on to the more exposed southern cliffs. The schist cliffs here are more thickly cloaked in plants than the serpentine ever is and their edges are softly bevelled with handsome craggy outcrops – home to the diminutive, rare and celebrated *Fringed Rupture-wort*.

Landewednack Church Cove
The church is thought to have been founded by the monks of Landévennec Abbey in Brittany (the name may be a simple transposition) and dedicated to their patron and abbot, St Winwalloe who we will meet again at Gunwalloe on the west coast of the Lizard.

Bass Point & Lloyds Signal Station
The story of the Lizard in modern times is one bound up with the story of communications – the pioneering development of telegraph, undersea telecom cables and radio are all represented in this one small area. Lizard Signal Station on Bass Point was built in 1872 by the shipping agents Fox & Company of Falmouth (the owners of Glendurgan on the Helford) so that inbound ships could communicate by semaphore flag with the station. When they arrived at Lizard Point ships may have been at sea for months without communication

with their owners. The ship owner could then be telegraphed and would in return relay orders to the captain about which markets were giving the best prices. Approaching Bass Point was itself a major cause of shipwreck

Housel Bay with the handsome schist crags of Pen Olver.

and stranding. In 1883 the operation was taken over by Lloyds of London. The red painted wall by the footpath is a shipping day mark and aligns with the building behind to identify the position of Vrogue Rock. Marconi set up the Lizard Wireless Station in 1901 to experiment with radio messaging. The original huts have been restored by the National Trust and are open in the summer.

The Mosel stops for an excursion

The 1882 story of the *Mosel* is a pleasing antidote to the tales of wreck and misfortune on the Lizard coast. Bound for America with 720 emigrants and crew, she steamed straight into Bass Point in thick fog and went aground directly under the signal station. Fortunately, she lay perfectly upright as if she had docked there on purpose. Passengers and crew disembarked along the bow sprite as if they were on an excursion.

A3083

Kynance
Cove Turn

Chapel Lane

Lizard
Town

Cross
Common

Cross

Tregaminion

Lloyd's Lane

Green Lane

Landewednack

Housel Bay Road

Lizard
Wireless
Station

Old Nuclear
Bunker

Pennenner Rd

Porthpean/Lighthouse Rd

Pystyll Lane

Housel
Bay

Laven-a-cean

Bolijack

Daws Ogo

Lion's Den Cave

Bumble Cove

Bumble Rock

Lizard
Point

Polpeor
Cove

Polbream
Cove

Lizard Lighthouse

Pen Olver

Polledan

Hansy 1911

Shag
Rock

Vellan Drang

Arab 1888

Gypsy Queen 1887

Labham
Reef

Pen Ervan

Enoch Rock

Nuovo Raffaelino 1872

Wandsbek 1900

Pelicanos 1853

The Dales

Vasiler

Mên Hyr

Suevic 1907

Polbarrow Arch
SS Bellucia
1917

Craggan
Rocks

Schist, gabbro & Kennack
gneiss make up a narrow
coastal fringe

Whale Rock

Parn Voose Cove

Balk Quarry
(serpentine, disused)

The Balk

Church Cove

Battleship Rock

Kilcobben Cove

Lizard Lifeboat Station

Prilla Cove

Hot Point

Hot Cove

Adolf Vinnen 1923

Pyg

Clan Malcolm 1935

Tregurra

SS Mosel 1882

Bass Point

Coastwatch Lookout
Lloyd's Signal Station
Cromdale 1913

Spernar
Shoals

Vrogue Rock

Czar 1859

Landewednack Schist
(recrystallised pillow lava & basalt)

Old Lizard Head Mica Schist
(recrystallised ocean sediments)

Walk 10
Housel Bay
• 5km (3 miles)
• 1–2 hours

0   0.25km   0.5km   0.75km   1km
0   ¼ mile   ½ mile

Housel Bay

The pioneer
undersea cable at
Housel Bay. The clip
is about 25cm wide.

To my mind, this is the best of Lizard beauty spots.
In 1872 this was the terminal for a pioneer undersea
communications cable between the Lizard and
Bilbao. The original cable is still clearly visible cut
into the cliff face. It only operated for four years
before a new cable had to be laid at Kennack Sands
because of damage caused by the rocky seabed.
I like the way it is fixed back to the cliff using gigantic
iron versions of the clips that fasten the telephone
cable in your own house.

The Suevic is broken

She ran aground in 1907 on the Mên Hyr rocks in poor visibility. The bow was badly damaged and impaled on the rocks but the rear section, with the engine room and most of the passenger cabins, was undamaged. Her bow was dynamited and, in what must surely rank as one of the most bizarre sights ever to pass up the English Channel, her rear section then steamed in reverse under her own power to Southampton where a new bow was fitted.

Lizard Point & Lighthouse

Sometimes welcomed as a first landfall after a long sea voyage, but all too often grimly surveyed by seamen who knew they were approaching their own graves. The reefs off Lizard Point snake out to sea ready to snare any passing ship that comes too close. At a time when ships navigated by the stars and often hugged the coast for safety, even patchy fog could be fatal. A severe storm could cost hundreds of lives. The lighthouse was built in 1752 to replace a failed private lighthouse built by the Falmouth privateer Sir John Killigrew. Sir John thought he could run a good scam by charging passing shipping for providing the light but he never managed to make it pay. Sir John and his family always lived on the edge of the law. His wife Lady Jane was a notorious pirate.

Flora

The south-facing cliffs & free-draining soils on the schist favour Lusitanian plants like *Fringed Rupture-wort*. It's found only on the British mainland at the Lizard. Dried & taken with wine it was thought to cure rupture or hernia – hence its Latin name *Herniaria ciliolata*. Also said to be efficacious on gonorrhoea & festulous ulcers, especially the sort that are foul & spreading. A big claim for a such a modest little plant. Look out for it on the path below the Lighthouse.

Fringed Rupture-wort

Babington's Leek at Housel Bay

Walk 11

Lizard Point, Pentreath & Kynance Cove

A jewel in a savage setting

Helston

Kynance

Landewednack
Lizard Point

BUS
Helston - Lizard Town bus, Lizard Town stop or jump off at Kynance Garage & walk across Lizard Downs to Kynance Cove.

PARKING
National Trust car parks at Lizard Point & above Kynance; there's a limited amount of free parking on The Green at Lizard Town.

FOOD & DRINKS
Well provided for in the season with cafes at Kynance Cove, Lizard Point & Lizard Town. Pub & food shops in Lizard Town.

LOOK OUT FOR...
- Choughs all along this coast
- Clovers from Lizard Point to Caerthillian Cove
- Pebbles at Pystyll Ogo
- Kynance Gate prehistoric village
- Serpentine pebbles & cliffs at Kynance

This is by far the most popular stretch of coast on the Lizard and it's full of delights and interest. These serpentine and schist cliffs take a fearful lashing in the winter – there's hardly a shrub, let alone a tree, to be seen. So it's all the more dazzling in the summer, when the turf blossoms with *Harebells*, *Bird's-foot Trefoil*, *Kidney Vetch*, daisies and clovers. Without doubt these are the most colourful cliffs in Cornwall.

Lizard Point
Lizard Point is mentioned as an important landmark on the tin trade route between the Mediterranean and Cornwall by Greek and Roman authors. More recently, it's been a communications hub with the maritime telegraph station at nearby Bass Point. The cafes at Lizard Point are often open in the winter so it's a great place to sit and watch the tail end of a gale blow through. The lifeboat station was sited here in the days when the lifeboats were powered only by oar and raw muscle – this was simply the nearest point to the main wrecking ground. When larger, motorised boats were introduced, the exposed position and lack of water at low tide restricted launching, so a new station was built at Kilcobben Cove.

Polpeor Cove

Pystyll Ogo & Pystyll Meadow
The grassy meadow here is the site of one of the most gruesome episodes in the long list of wrecks on the Lizard reefs. *HMS Royal Anne* was a Royal Navy galley, powered by oars as well a sails.

Kynance Cove

She was on her way to protect the West Africa slave trade from pirates when, in November 1721, she sailed into a gale in the Western Approaches. She was driven backwards towards the Lizard finally going aground on the Stags where she disintegrated so rapidly that people were thrown directly from their hammocks into the sea. More than 200 people lost their lives; most are buried in shallow pits on the low cliff and meadow above Pystyll Ogo where the bodies came ashore. Over the following weeks there were reports of stray dogs feasting on the bodies and for many years after that, horrified locals would stone any stray dog they came across. There's a little path down to the beach where, under the small waterfall (Cornish: *Pystyll* is *waterfall*, *ogo* is *cave*) you can pick up beautiful pebbles – mainly basalt, Man O'War Gneiss and Old Lizard Head schists. In the autumn seals give birth in the more secluded caves and choughs also breed here in the summer.

Flora

The cliffs here are very exposed to gales & are kept closely trimmed by both rabbits & wind. *Spring Squill* & *Sea Campion* get the show going, followed by a dazzling summer display when the turf blossoms with *Harebells, Bird's-foot Trefoil, Kidney Vetch*, daisies & clovers. These cliffs are without doubt the most colourful in Cornwall. *Bloody Cranesbill* grows on scree slopes on the path down to Kynance Cove.

Wild Thyme

Thyme Broomrape

Pentreath Beach & Caerthillian Valley

This beach, exposed at low water, has become a little difficult to access because of rock falls on the old path west of Carn Caerthillian. The easiest way to get onto the beach now is to scramble down the low cliffs around Caerthillian Cove. A popular beach with surfers.

Kynance Cove

Idealised by romantic painters and poets in the C18th and C19th, it's a sublime arrangement of untamed and savage nature in a picturesque arrangement of islands, cliffs and sand. Try to arrive when the tide is falling as many of the caves, with their beautiful naturally polished walls, are inaccessible at high water.

Kynance Gate Prehistoric Village

This is a rare chance on the Lizard to walk around a prehistoric settlement. It dates from the Bronze Age about 3,200 years ago and was occupied for three or four hundred years. It was probably a summer settlement as there aren't any fields nearby. The southern group of huts is grouped around a prominent natural outcrop of serpentine with an inclined stone set at its centre – a little reminiscent of the central stone at Boscawen-ûn Circle near Penzance. A later, northern group of five houses are difficult to make out once the summer vegetation has taken hold. An information board at the site has more information. There's a strong visual link with a prominent barrow on the skyline to the northeast. You can walk to it from here.

Kynance Farm

Quarry rock/ tite)

Prehistoric barrow on skyline

Kissing gate

Permissive path linking Lizard Downs & Windmill Farm Nature Reserve

Kynance Garage

Grochall Farm

Mile End

If you're arriving by bus you could jump off at Kynance Garage & walk across Lizard Downs

Kynance Gate
Prehistoric Village

Kynance

Dead end path

Kynance Brook

Kynance North Valley

L i z a r d   D o w n s

Goose Curtain Brook

Kynance South Valley

37

reaks ugh cks

Kynance Heights

A3083

Kynance Cove Turn

Lawarnick Pit

Lawarnick Cove

Tor Balk

P e n t r e a t h   C l i f f

Carn Goon

Chapel Lane

Lizard Town

ll ve

Asparagus Island

The Devil's Letterbox
Gull Rock

The Bishop

Kynance Cove

Yellow Carn

Holestrow

P

P

Serpentine

Lion Rock

Enys Vean

Maud 1912
Boiler visible at low tide

Carn Caerthillian

Pentreath Lane

GOONHILLY SHEET

MAN O'WAR SHEET
500 million year old rocks that predate the creation of the Rheic Ocean

Pentreath Beach

Caerthillian Cove

Lizard Head Lane

Landewednack Schist
(recrystallised pillow lava & basalt)

Crane Ledges

Holseer Cove

Scathe
Venton Hill Point

Pystyll Lane

Penmenner Rd

Porthgeyr/Lighthouse Rd

Old Lizard Head Schists
(recrystallised ocean sediments)

Suffolk 1886

Old Lizard Head

Xanthus 1841
Quadrant

HMS Royal Anne 1721
Queen Margret 1913

Mulvin   **Stags**

Taylor's Rock

Eltyenburgh 1854

Clanker Drang

Lead Pool

Pystyll Meadow

Pystyll Ogo

Lizard Point

Polpeor Cove

Shag Rock

Lizard Point

P

Polbrean Cove

Arab 1888

Man of War Gneiss & granite
(Heavily deformed granite rocks from the Gondwanian plate that crashed into Cornwall)

Man O'War

Mên Par
Labham Rock

Yellan Drang

Labham Reef

Gypsy Qu

Pen Er

Clidgas Rocks
or The Cledges

Pelicanos 1853

The Dales

Vasiler   Mên Hyr

Suevic 1907

Walk 11
Lizard & Kynance
- 7km (4¼ miles)
- 2–3 hours

0	0.25km	0.5km	0.75km	1km

0	¼ mile	½ mile

Walks in this book

1	Roskilly's Stroll	3.1km (2 miles) 1–2 hours	🚌 **Helston–St Keverne bus (36)** St Keverne Square stop then walk to Roskilly's along Trelyn Lane.
2	Lowland Point	8.2km (5 miles) 3–4 hours	🚌 **Helston–St Keverne bus (36)** Coverack bus shelter, North Corner stop.
3	Chynhalls Stroll from Coverack	2.6km (1½ miles) 1–2 hours	🚌 **Helston–St Keverne bus (36)** Coverack bus shelter, North Corner stop.
4	Coverack, Black Head & Downas Cove	6.3km (4 miles) 3–4 hours	🚌 **Helston–St Keverne bus (36)** Coverack bus shelter, North Corner, 4 car park spaces at Treleaver.
5	Kennack Sands to Lankidden Cove	4.7km (3 miles) 1–2 hours	🚌 **Helston–Lizard bus (37)** Kuggar stop. 🚌 **Helston–St Keverne bus (36)** Coverack bus shelter, North Corner stop.
6	Goonhilly Downs, Dry Tree stroll	4km (2½ miles) 1–2 hours	🚌 **Helston–St Keverne bus (36)** Goonhilly Earth Station stop. National Nature Reserve & car park is just south of Earth Station.
7	Goonhilly & Erisey	8.8km (5½ miles) 3–4 hours	🚌 **Helston–St Keverne bus (36)** Goonhilly Earth Station stop. National Nature Reserve & car park is just south of Earth Station.
8	Erisey, Poltesco & Carleon Cove	5.8km (3½ miles) 2–3 hours	🚌 **Helston–Lizard bus (37)** Ask to get off at Polstangey Bridge
9	Poltesco Stroll	1.6km (1 mile) 1 hour	🚌 **Helston–Lizard bus (37)** Ruan Minor stop & walk down Poltesco Lane
10	Landewednack, Housel Bay & Lizard Point	5km (3 miles) 1–2 hours	🚌 **Helston–Lizard bus (37)** Tregaminion or Lizard Green stops
11	Lizard Point, Pentreath & Kynance Cove	7km (4¼ miles) 2–3 hours	🚌 **Helston–Lizard bus (37)** Lizard Green stop or jump off at Kynance Garage & walk across Lizard Downs.